SIRT FOOD DIET

A Meal Plan with Quick, Easy, and Proven Ways to Activate Your "Skinny Gene" To Burn Fat, Get Lean, and Stay Healthy Maintaining lifestyle

BY

SARAH WHITE

information contained within this document, including, but not limited to, - errors, omissions, or inaccuracies.

Contents

INTRODUCTION 7

CHINESE RECIPES: DUCK NOODLE SOUP 16

CHINESE SPINACH SALAD 19

APPLE BUCKWHEAT PANCAKES WITH COCONUT CARAMEL APPLES 21

QUICK VEGAN BREAKFAST BURRITOS............................ 23

CHICKPEA OMELETTE.. 25

GINGERBREAD WAFFLES 26

JELLY-FILLED MUFFINS.. 28

TOAST WITH REFRIED BEANS AND AVOCADO 30

SUN-DRIED TOMATO, MUSHROOM, AND SPINACH TOFU QUICHE 31

VEGAN BREAKFAST SANDWICH.................................. 33

WARM AND NUTTY CINNAMON QUINOA 34

CANAL HOUSE LENTILS 36

HOT CHOCOLATE BANANA-NUT OATMEAL 37

PEANUT BUTTER BANANA BREAD GRANOLA 39

BROCCOLI AND QUINOA BREAKFAST PATTIES 41

SALTED CARAMEL APPLE BREAKFAST BARS 43

SWEET POTATO BREAKFAST BOWL 46

GRITS BOWL WITH AVOCADO AND BAKED TOFU STRIPS............... 47

GREEK CHICKPEAS ON TOAST 49

BREAKFAST HASH 51

SPINACH ARTICHOKE QUICHE.................................... 53

FRIED TOFU 55

BREAKFAST TURMERIC TOFU 56

DELI-STYLE VEGAN CREAM CHEESE BOWLS 58

CARDAMOM AND PEACH QUINOA PORRIDGE 59

BANANA SMASH OATMEAL 1

SIX PLANTS BASED OIL-FREE SALAD DRESSING.................................... 2

FUSION LUNCH BURRITOS 5

AVOCADO HUMMUS BOWL... 8

SLOW COOKER PUMPKIN CHILI... 10

BUTTERNUT SQUASH & AND CRANBERRY QUINOA SALAD 11

HERBED WILD RICE STUFFED POTATOES 12

SPICY KALE SALAD WITH CHICKPEAS AND MAPLE DIJON DRESSING.............. 14

GLUTEN-FREE MANGO AND BLACK BEAN TACOS 16

SPICY KALE SALAD WITH CHICKPEAS AND MAPLE DIJON DRESSING.............. 18

OLD-FASHIONED POTATO SALAD 20

THREE BEAN SALAD 23

GREEK CHICKEN, TOMATO & FETA BAKE... 24

BUTTERNUT & LEEK SOUP.. 26

CHICKEN VINAIGRETTE.. 28

HEARTY BEEF STEW WITH MUSHROOMS AND MASH 31

EASY SEAFOOD BREYANI WITH PRAWNS, HAKE AND CALAMARI................. 33

PORTUGUESE-STYLE CHICKEN 35

CHEF WENDY 37

BAKE DINNER... 42

VEGETABLE FRIED RICE RECIPES 44

MEXICAN HEALTHY DINNERS 46

FAIRHAVEN FISH CHOWDER 48

PASTA SALAD... 50

BUFFALO CHICKEN WINGS 51

INTRODUCTION

The Sirtfood Diet regimen breakthroughs healthy and balanced nutrition; nevertheless, it is excessive in calories and also food choices. It likewise includes alcohol consumption loads of juice, which is not a healthy suggestion. Sirtfoods are practically all healthy and balanced choices and may even bring about some health and wellness benefits as a result of their cell support or mitigating homes. Nonetheless, eating only several exceptionally healthy nourishments can not fulfill the whole of your body's wholesome needs. The Sirtfood Diet plan is superfluously excessive and provides no noticeable, distinct health and wellness advantages over a few other sorts of diet plans.

Also, consuming only 1,000 calories is routinely not suggested without the supervision of a physician. In any event, consuming 1,500 calories for each day is unnecessarily prohibitive for some individuals. The diet plan likewise needs draining to three eco-friendly juices for each day. Although juices can be a respectable root of nutrients and minerals, they are likewise a root of sugar. Also, they include virtually none of the healthy fiber that whole foods are expanded from the ground.

Likewise, sampling on juice throughout the day is not a practical concept for both your sugar and your teeth. Also, because the diet regimen is constrained in calories and food choice, it is higher than likely inadequate in healthy protein, nutrients, and minerals, particularly during the main stage. Due to the low-calorie degrees as well as excessive food choices, this diet could be tough to abide by for the whole three weeks. Include that to the enormous start expenditures of acquiring a juicer, guide, and certain unusual and expensive ingredients, just as the time costs of preparing explicit dinners and juices, and this diet plan obtains unfeasible and not practical for some people. While it may not be a diet plan that is healthy to adhere to correctly, there are many legitimate reasons to integrate wide varieties of the center sirtfoods in a weight-reduction project, consisting of kale, berries, ginger, turmeric, eco-friendly tea as well as olive oil.

You will shed optimal weight if you follow this diet plan purely. "Regardless of whether you're consuming 1,000 calories of tacos, 1,000 calories of kale, or 1,000 calories of snickerdoodles, you will drop weight at 1,000 calories!" states Dr. Youdim. Be that as it may, she furthermore raises that you can have accomplishment with a gradually practical calorie constraint. The common each day caloric admission of someone out a limited consuming routine is 2,000 to 2,200, so reducing to 1,500 is yet restricting and also would certainly be a compelling weight reduction strategy for many, she says.

This diet may help you obtain a lot more in shape, given that it is low in calories, yet the weight is probably most likely to return once the food shuts. The menu is too brief, even to consider having a dragged out impact on your wellness. The creators of the Sirtfood Diet plan make uncommon instances, including that the diet plan can super-charge weight reduction, turn on your "slim gene," as well as deter health issues.

The issue is there isn't a lot of verification to back them.

Up until this factor, there's no encouraging evidence that the Sirtfood Diet regimen has a better influence on weight decrease than a few other calorie-confined diet regimens. What's more, albeit a significant great deal of these nourishments has healthy buildings, there has not been any type of drawn-out human evaluation to decide if eating a diet abundant in sirtfoods has any kind of distinct health advantages. Soon, the Sirtfood Diet book reports the consequences of a pilot study led by the writers and consisting of 39 participants from their wellness neighborhood. Regardless, the results of this assessment appear not to have been dispersed anywhere else.

For a multi-week, the participants complied with the diet as well as practiced each day. Toward the week's end, members lost a regular of 7 pounds (3.2 kg) and kept up or even grabbed the mass.

Nonetheless, these results are not surprising. Limiting your calorie admission to 1,000 calories and practicing simultaneously will practically consistently trigger weight decrease. Regardless, this kind of rapid weight decrease is neither certifiable nor long-lasting. This investigation did not comply with members after the initial week to check whether they brought back any one of the weights, which is generally the circumstance.

At the point when your body is vigor denied, it undergoes its dilemma vigor stores, or glycogen, notwithstanding eating fat and also muscle mass.

Every atom of glycogen needs 3-- 4 particles of water to be done away with. At the point when your body experiences glycogen, it takes care of this water also. It's called "water weight." In the initial seven day stretch of outrageous calorie limitation, just around 33% of the weight reduction stems from fat, while the other 66% originates from water, muscle, and glycogen. When your calorie admission builds, your body restores its glycogen shops, and the weight returns right. Tragically, this sort of calorie constraint can likewise make your body lower its metabolic price, causing you to need much fewer calories every day for vitality than formerly. Probably, this diet regimen might aid you in losing a couple of extra pounds initially.

Nonetheless, it will probably return when the food is ended up. To the level of forestalling sickness, three weeks is most likely not long sufficient to have any type of measurable long-haul persuade. However, adding Sirt foods to your regular diet plan over the long haul could simply be a wise idea. Yet, you ought to avoid food selection and start doing that now.

Some Healthy Sirtfoods

There's no refuting that sirtfoods are beneficial for you. They are frequently high in nutrients and also brimming with healthy plant mixes. Besides, contemplates have connected a considerable lot of the sustenance suggested on the Sirtfood Diet plan with health and wellness benefits.

1. Chia Seeds

In the world of sirtfoods, chia seeds are noted to be a moderate Sirtuins-actuating food that the authors of The Sirtfood Diet show in their publication as what might be contrasted to going for a stroll instead of entering a severe sweating meeting at the rec center.

There's no reputable proof to help this instance. However, there's no conversation that chia seeds load a tremendous quantity of sustenance into a little package, making them a skillful approach to accumulate on crucial nutrients like fiber (around 10 grams for every ounce) and folate (about 14 micrograms), per the USDA. Chia is likewise an edible root of plant protein. Just spray the seeds over a healthy smoothie dish, contribute to healthy smoothies or blend right into grain.

2. Cinnamon

In an examination distributed in April 2017 in Biochemistry And Biology and Molecular Biology, experts made use of a COMPUTER model to examine whether cinnamon passed Sirtuins and discovered encouraging associations. This does not show anything yet, yet it's a remarkable structure block for the future research study. However, regardless of every little thing, cinnamon makes the sirtfoods checklist because it provides ground-breaking polyphenols, which are plant blends with cancer-avoidance representatives, and also mitigating residential properties. What's more, some assessment seems to advise that cinnamon can help control blood sugar levels by reducing back carbohydrate handling and improving exactly how the body responds to insulin, according to the Mayo Facility. Cinnamon goes amazing in espresso, warm chocolate, collard greens, prepared squash, soups, healthy smoothies, and also passion massages for lean pork.

3. Cocoa

The recommended Sirtuins-enacting supplement in chocolate is epicatechin, a superb sort of cell reinforcement furthermore discovered in tea and grapes. As a polyphenol-rich food, cocoa may aid advancement healthy bloodstream, per an April 2017 Cochrane survey-- not that you needed one more inspiration to appreciate chocolate. Merely recollect that the benefits are from the cacao plant, not all the extra sugar, salt, and fat is ready pleasant deals. Look for one of the most raised price dull chocolate you can find to get one of the most rewards.

4. Olive Oil

The supposed Sirtuins-initiating polyphenols in added virgin olive oil are oleuropein and hydroxytyrosol. See to it that olive oil is a vital part of the heart-healthy Sirtfood diet plan, which can furthermore bolster a weight-the board strategy. It's also affluent in monounsaturated fats, which can assist enhance cholesterol degrees, specifically when they supplant hydrogenated fat or fine-tuned carbs, per the American Heart Association.

5. Berries

Berries, for example, raspberries, strawberries, and blackberries are abundant in polyphenols, so it shocks nobody that seeds are cancer cells prevention agent whizzes, per the Mayo Clinic. They're additionally plentiful in fiber and nutrient C. New berries are outstanding all alone, and also strengthened berries can be favorably delighted in all year in a group pleasing smoothie mix or an unexpectedly new salsa.

6. Kale

A mug of kale has twofold the day's nutrient An and more nutrition C than an orange, per the USDA. To get ready, kale, leave stems, layer, and cut transversely into strips (chiffonade) before working for several moments with your favored dressing. Consist of these seasoned kale strips as well as whatever organic item you have around with your much-loved grain, for instance, farro, wheat berry, sorghum, or freekeh, for a snappy and healthy whole grain serving of blended greens.

7. Red Wine

A red wine made its name in health hovers for containing the polyphenol resveratrol. An observational study in individuals proposes that half-price admission can have health benefits for heart wellness and potentially for life span and psychological wellness, too, as indicated by Harvard Health Posting. As a traditional part of the Sirtfood Diet plan, it's planned to be thrilled with food in appropriate amounts (e.g., one 5-ounce glass for ladies every day). It's not directly for everybody, as well as there are numerous various strategies to eat and drink for good wellness for any type of person who wants to keep away from red wine whatsoever, form, or kind.

CHINESE RECIPES: DUCK NOODLE SOUP

Ingredients:

- 2 confit duck legs, from a jar

- 1 tbsp clear honey

- 1 tsp chinese five spice

- 1 tbsp soy sauce

- 1 tsp sesame oil

- 100 g egg noodles

- ½ litres chicken stock

- 2 tbsp oyster sauce

- 1 tbsp sesame oil

- 4 spring onions, sliced

- some watercress

Directions:

1. **Duck noodle soup** is a delicious recipe you can try at home and it's straightforward to make. First of all, we will scrape off any excess fat from the duck legs with a knife. We do this to prevent the soup from becoming too greasy.

2. Next, taking a bowl, we'll mix the honey, the Chinese five-spice powder and half of the soya sauce.

3. After, heat a pan over a medium hob and place the duck legs in the hot pan. Pour the honey mixture over the duck legs and cook gently until sticky and glossy. Now, we'll remove the duck legs from the pan and shred the meat.

4. Bring a saucepan full of water to the boil and cook the noodles with a pinch of salt until tender. Drain the noodles well in a colander.

5. Next, heat the ½ liters of chicken stock in a large saucepan and add the remaining soy sauce, oyster sauce and sesame oil and stir to combine. Add some salt to taste.

6. Lastly, put in the spring onions, noodles and duck meat.

   To serve the **duck noodle soup**, divide it among two bowls and garnish with some watercress.

CHINESE SPINACH SALAD

Salad

- 3 heads fresh spinach, washed and drained
- 1 cup water chestnuts, sliced
- 3 eggs, hard boiled, sliced
- 1 cup fresh bean sprouts
- 4 slices bacon, cooked and crumbled (optional)

For the dressing

- 1 cup sunflower oil
- 3/4 cup chopped onion
- 1/4 cup red wine vinegar
- 1/2 cup sugar
- 1 tsp salt
- 1/3 cup catsup
- 1 tablespoon Worcestershire sauce or soy sauce if you're a vegetarian

Directions:

1. **Chinese spinach salad** is totally delicious and very healthy. Spinach is not everyone's cup of tea but it has a high nutritional value and is extremely rich in antioxidants, iron, vitamin A, and calcium.

2. To make our spinach salad which is ideal as a starter or as part of the main course, we will first mix all of the dressing ingredients and refrigerate.

3. Now, we will mix the salad ingredients. It's best to use fresh spinach as it retains all its nutritional value. Arrange well, placing the spinach first, then topping off with the chestnuts, bean sprouts and finally with the hard-boiled eggs arranged on top as in the photo. If you are vegetarian, you can leave off the bacon slices!

Just before serving, toss the salad with the dressing and our healthy Chinese spinach salad is ready to serve our hungry guests!

APPLE BUCKWHEAT PANCAKES WITH COCONUT CARAMEL APPLES

Cook Time: 60 minutes

1. **Servings:** 11 pancakes Apple Buckwheat Pancakes With Coconut Caramel Apples

Ingredients:

- 1 3/4 cups buckwheat flour
- 4 tablespoon coconut sugar
- 2 teaspoon baking powder
- 1/4 teaspoon vanilla powder
- 3 teaspoons cinnamon
- 1/4 teaspoon sea salt
- 2 tablespoons + 1 teaspoon coconut oil, melted
- 1 1/4 cups + 2 tablespoons almond milk
- 1 tablespoon flax seeds and 3 tablespoons water
- 1 cup apple chunks
- 1/4 teaspoon water
- 1 apple, peeled and cut into wedges

Instructions:

1. Prepare flax egg by mixing flax seeds and water. Let rest for 5 minutes. Add flour, baking powder, 2 tablespoons coconut sugar, vanilla powder, salt, and 2 teaspoons cinnamon to a bowl.

2. Mix flax egg with 1 1/4 cups almond milk and add to dry ingredients. Let pancake batter rest for 15 minutes. Add 2 tablespoon almond milk, chopped apple, and coconut oil.

3. Add few drops of coconut oil to a pan over medium-low heat and spread. Add 1/4 cup batter to it and cook for 3 minutes. Flip and cook for 2 minutes.

4. Add 1 teaspoon coconut oil, remaining coconut sugar, cinnamon and water in a pan. Mix and combine until smooth. Add apple wedges and cook until soft to make coconut caramel apples.

5. Serve caramel apples over pancakes.

QUICK VEGAN BREAKFAST BURRITOS

Cook Time: 30 minutes

Servings: 2 burritos

Ingredients:

- 1 1/2 cups water
- 3/4 cup white rice, rinsed and drained
- 1/2 + 1 lime juice
- 1/4 cup cilantro, chopped
- 1/2 teaspoon salt
- 1/2 red onion
- 4 red potatoes
- 2 tablespoons vegan butter
- 1/4 teaspoon black pepper
- 1 cup black beans, cooked
- 1/4 teaspoon chili, cumin and garlic powder
- 1/4 avocado
- 1 jalapeno, seeds removed and sliced
- 1 cup cabbage, sliced
- 2 vegan flour tortillas
- 1/4 cup salsa

Instructions:

1. Add rice, water, and 1/4 teaspoon salt to a pot and bring to boil. Reduce the heat to low, cover and cook for 20 minutes. Remove and set aside.

2. Wash and chop potatoes. Cut onion to 1/4" rings. Heat a skillet over medium heat. Add vegan butter and coat. Add potatoes to one side and onions to others. Season and cover and cook for 5 minutes on one side and 5 minutes on other. Remove and set aside.

3. Add beans to a pan placed over medium heat and season with garlic powder, cumin, and chili powder. Once bubbles form, reduce heat.

4. Mix avocado and 1 lime juice in a bowl. Add jalapeno and cabbage and mix. Season and set coleslaw aside. Add lime juice and cilantro to rice and toss.

5. Wrap tortillas in a towel and microwave for 30 seconds.

6. Add fillings in it, avocado and salsa. Roll into burritos, slice and serve.

CHICKPEA OMELETTE

Cook Time: 5 minutes

Servings: 1

Ingredients:

- 3 tablespoons chickpea flour
- 8 tablespoons water
- 2 tablespoons oil
- 1 onion
- fresh herbs, to taste
- 1/2 teaspoon salt
- A pinch of black pepper

Instructions:

1. Combine flour with salt and pepper. Add water and mix until batter forms. Add herbs and onions in it. Mix well.
2. Heat oil in a pan. Add batter to it and spread evenly. Cook for a few minutes. Flip and cook until done.
3. Remove from heat and serve.

GINGERBREAD WAFFLES

Cook Time: 15 minutes**Servings:** 6

Ingredients:

- 1 tablespoon flax seeds
- 1 cup spelt flour
- 2 teaspoons baking powder
- 1 1/2 teaspoons cinnamon
- 4 tablespoons coconut sugar
- 2 teaspoons ginger
- 1/4 teaspoon salt
- 1/4 teaspoon baking soda
- 1 tablespoon apple cider vinegar
- 1 cup nondairy milk

- 2 tablespoons blackstrap molasses
- 1 1/2 tablespoons oil

Instructions:

1. Grease and preheat the waffle iron.
2. Mix flax seeds, flour, baking powder, cinnamon, coconut sugar, ginger, salt and baking soda in a bowl and stir well to combine.
3. Mix the remaining ingredients in a separate bowl and stir well. Add wet ingredients to dry ones and mix until just combined.
4. Add the mixture to the waffle maker and cook as per the instructions. Serve and enjoy.

JELLY-FILLED MUFFINS

Cook Time: 25 minutes

Servings: 12

Ingredients:

- 3/4 teaspoon baking powder
- 1 1/2 cups all-purpose flour
- 1/2 teaspoon baking soda
- 1/2 teaspoon ground nutmeg
- 1 cup plain soy milk
- 1 teaspoon cider vinegar
- 3/4 cup and 2 tablespoons granulated sugar
- 2 tablespoons cornstarch
- 1/3 cup vegetable oil
- 2 teaspoons vanilla extract
- 1/3 cup strawberries jam
- 1/2 teaspoon fine salt

Instructions:

1. Heat oven to 350F. Line a muffin cup with paper liners and set aside.
2. Add baking soda, baking powder, flour, salt and nutmeg to a bowl. Make a well in the mixture.

3. Mix milk, cornstarch and vinegar in another bowl until cornstarch dissolves. Add to the well in the flour mixture. Add vanilla, oil and sugar and stir well.

4. Fill each muffin cup to three quarters. Create indentation by spreading batter slightly from middle to edges. Add 1 teaspoon jam into the well. Repeat with each.

5. Bake for 22 minutes. Let cool on a wire rack for 5 minutes. Remove, cool completely and serve.

TOAST WITH REFRIED BEANS AND AVOCADO

Cook Time: 5 minutes

Servings: 2

Ingredients:

- 1 cup vegan refried beans
- 2 sandwich bread slices
- 1 avocado, sliced
- Salt, to taste
- white onion, sliced

Instructions:

1. Toast the bread slices. Add avocado and beans on top.
2. Add onions and sprinkle salt over it.
3. Serve and enjoy!

SUN-DRIED TOMATO, MUSHROOM, AND SPINACH TOFU QUICHE

Cook Time: 50 minutes

Servings: 8

Ingredients:

- 1 cup almonds, grounded
- 1 tablespoon flax seeds + 3 tablespoon water, mixed
- 1 cup rolled oats, grounded
- 2 teaspoons dried oregano
- 1 teaspoon dried parsley
- 2 tablespoons olive oil
- 3 tablespoons water
- 1/2 teaspoon kosher salt
- 14 oz firm tofu
- 1 leek, sliced
- 3 garlic cloves, minced
- 3 cups cremini mushrooms, sliced
- 1/2 cup basil leaves, chopped
- 1/2 cup chives, chopped
- 1 cup baby spinach
- 1/3 cup oil-packed-sun dried tomatoes, chopped

- 2 tablespoons yeast
- 1 teaspoon sea salt

Instructions:

1. Preheat the oven to 350F and grease a tart pan. Drain water from the tofu completely.

2. Whisk flax and water in a bowl and let rest for 5 minutes: Mix oat flour, almond meal, parsley, 1 teaspoon oregano, and kosher salt in a bowl. Add 1 tablespoon oil and flax mixture. Stir until dough forms.

3. Add dough to the pan and spread evenly on the bottom. Poke some holes in it. Bake crust for 16 minutes, let cool, and increase oven temp to 375F.

4. Add tofu into a blender. Blend until smooth. Cook garlic and onion in a pan over medium heat for few minutes add mushrooms, season, and cook over medium-high for 12 minutes. Add herbs, yeast, spinach, tomatoes, salt, and oregano and combine well. Cook until spinach wilts.

5. Remove and mix in tofu. Add on top of the baked crust and smooth out. Bake for 37 minutes. Cool for 10 minutes and serve.

VEGAN BREAKFAST SANDWICH

Cook Time: 15 minutes

Servings: 1

Ingredients:

- 1 vegan sausage patty
- 1 English muffin
- 1 slice vegan cheese
- 1 teaspoon strawberry jam
- 1 teaspoon hot sauce
- 1/4 avocado, sliced

Instructions:

1. Toast the muffin well. Cook the patty in microwave for 1 minute. Add cheese on top and heat for 30 seconds.
2. Slice the toasted muffin and add spread the jam on top. Add patty and cheese. Add avocado. Serve and enjoy.

WARM AND NUTTY CINNAMON QUINOA

Cook Time: 20 minutes

Servings: 4

Ingredients:

- 1 cup of water
- 1 cup 1% low-fat milk, organic
- 2 cups blackberries
- 1 cup quinoa, organic
- 1/3 cup pecans, chopped and toasted
- 1/2 teaspoon cinnamon
- 4 teaspoons organic agave nectar

Instructions:

1. Mix water, quinoa, and milk in a pan. Bring to a boil over high heat. Reduce the heat, cover and cook for 15 minutes. Turn heat off and let sit for 5 minutes.

2. Add cinnamon and blackberries and transfer to 4 bowls. Add pecans. Add 1 teaspoon agave over each bowl. Serve and enjoy.

CANAL HOUSE LENTILS

Cook Time: 1 hour

Servings: 8

Ingredients:

- 1 leek, white and green parts, chopped
- 2 tablespoons olive oil
- 1 tablespoon tomato paste
- 1 garlic clove, sliced
- 1 cup green lentils
- 2 tablespoons soy sauce
- salt and pepper, to taste

Instructions:

1. Heat oil in a pan over medium heat. Add garlic, leek and tomato sauce and cook for 4 minutes.
2. Add 2 1/2 cups water and lentils. Bring to a boil. Reduce the heat, cover and cook for 55 minutes.
3. Remove from heat and let sit for 10 minutes. Add soy sauce and season to taste. Serve and enjoy.

HOT CHOCOLATE BANANA-NUT OATMEAL

Cook Time: 25 minutes

Servings: 4

Ingredients:

- 2 cups almond milk
- 1/4 teaspoon almond extract
- 2 ripe bananas (1 1/2 diced and 1 1/2 slices crosswise)
- 2 cups rolled oats
- 1/4 teaspoon vanilla extract
- 2 tablespoons cocoa powder
- 1/3 cup walnuts, toasted and chopped
- 2 tablespoons honey
- 2 tablespoons milk chocolate chips
- A pinch cinnamon

Instructions:

1. Add 1 3/4 cups water, almond milk, almond and vanilla extracts, diced bananas and pinch of salt to a pan and bring to a boil over high heat.
2. Add cocoa powder, oats and 1 tablespoon honey and reduce heat to medium. Cook for 7 minutes.

3. Transfer to 4 bowls and top with sliced bananas, honey, walnuts, chocolate chips and cinnamon. Serve and enjoy.

PEANUT BUTTER BANANA BREAD GRANOLA

Cook Time: 50 minutes

Servings: 6 cups

Ingredients:

- 3 cups rolled oats
- 1 cup salted peanuts
- 1 cup banana chips, crushed lightly
- 1/4 cup brown sugar
- 1/2 cup uncooked quinoa
- 1 teaspoon cinnamon
- 6 tablespoons butter, unsalted
- 1/3 cup peanut butter
- 1/4 cup pure honey
- 2 teaspoons vanilla extract
- 1/2 cup banana, mashed
- 1 teaspoon salt

Instructions:

1. Preheat the oven to 325F and line 2 rimmed baking sheets with parchment paper. Mix banana chips, peanuts, oats, sugar, quinoa, cinnamon, and salt in a bowl.

2. Heat peanut butter, butter, and honey in a pan over medium-low heat for 4 minutes. Remove from heat and add vanilla and banana. Add to the oat mixture and mix well.

3. Spread granola onto the baking sheet — Bake for 27 minutes.

4. Cool on wire racks. Serve and enjoy

BROCCOLI AND QUINOA BREAKFAST PATTIES

Cook Time: 25 minutes

Servings: 8

Ingredients:

- 2 cups vegetable broth
- 1 cup cooked quinoa
- 1 cup broccoli and carrots mixture, shredded
- 2 flax eggs
- 2 garlic cloves, minced
- 1/2 cup breadcrumbs, gluten-free
- 1 1/2 teaspoons garlic powder
- 2 teaspoons parsley
- 1 1/2 teaspoons onion powder
- 2 tablespoons coconut oil
- Salt and pepper, to taste

Instructions:

1. Rinse quinoa and add to a pan with vegetable broth. Once it boils, reduce the heat and cook for 15 minutes.

2. Add quinoa, flax eggs, shredded broccoli and carrots, garlic, parsley, breadcrumbs, 2 tablespoons oil, salt, and pepper to a bowl and mix well to combine.

3. Add little olive oil to the pan. Shape the mixture into balls and place them on the pan and flatten with the palm of your hand — Cook for 3 minutes per side.

4. Top with parsley and serve. Enjoy!

SALTED CARAMEL APPLE BREAKFAST BARS

Cook time: 30 minutes

Servings: 10 bars

Ingredients:

- 1 cup rolled oats
- 1 cup oat flour
- 1 teaspoon baking powder
- 2 apples, grated
- 3/4 cup medjol dates, pitted
- 3 tablespoon chia seeds
- 2/3 cup tahini
- 1 teaspoon vanilla extract
- 1/4 cup + 2 tablespoon plant milk
- 1/2 teaspoon salt

Instructions:

1. Preheat the oven to 350F. Mix baking powder, oats, oat flour and salt in a bowl. Mix well to combine. Add grated apples to a bowl.

2. Add tahini, dates, chia seeds, milk and vanilla extract to a blender and blend until smooth. Add the date mixture and grated apples to the bowl with dry ingredients. Stir well.

3. Transfer the batter to a greased baking pan and bake for 30 minutes. Let cool for 10 minutes in the pan.

4. Remove, let cool completely, slice and serve. Enjoy!

SWEET POTATO BREAKFAST BOWL

Cook Time: 1 hour 25 minutes

Servings: 2

Ingredients:

- 16 oz. sweet potato
- 2 tablespoons raisins
- 2 tablespoons almond butter
- 2 tablespoons chopped nuts
- Cinnamon, to taste

Instructions:

1. Preheat the oven to 375F. Poke potatoes with a fork and wrap in foil. Bake for 80 minutes. Let cool for 5 minutes and peel.
2. Mash the potatoes in a bowl, add cinnamon. Add to a bowl, top with raisins and nuts. Add almond butter. Serve and enjoy!

GRITS BOWL WITH AVOCADO AND BAKED TOFU STRIPS

Cook Time: 45 minutes

Servings: 4

Ingredients:

- 1/4 cup soy sauce
- 1 block tofu, sliced into strips
- 1/2 teaspoon onion powder
- 1 tablespoon olive oil
- 1 teaspoon turmeric
- 4 servings grits
- 1/2 cup nutritional yeast
- 1 avocado
- 2 tablespoons vegan margarine
- salt and pepper, to taste

Instructions:

1. Preheat the oven to 425F. Mix turmeric, soy sauce, olive oil, and onion powder in a bowl and toss with tofu strips. Let rest for 15 minutes.
2. Place the tofu strips on a lined baking sheet — Bake for 15 minutes on both sides.

3. Cook grits according to package directions and finish cooking when tofu is done. Add margarine and yeast and divide among 4 bowls.

4. Add 1/4 baked tofu strips, 1/4 avocado, and 1/4 tomatoes to each bowl. Season and serve.

GREEK CHICKPEAS ON TOAST

Cook Time: 35 minutes

Servings: 2

Ingredients:

- 3 shallots, diced
- 2 tablespoons olive oil
- 2 garlic cloves, diced
- 1/2 teaspoon cinnamon
- 1/2 teaspoon sweet paprika
- 1/4 teaspoon smoked paprika
- 1/2 teaspoon salt
- 2 large tomatoes, skinned
- 6 slices crusty bread, toasted
- 2 cups chickpeas, cooked
- A pinch of black pepper
- Kalamata olives, for serving

Instructions:

1. Heat oil on a pan over medium heat and fry shallots until done. Add garlic and cook until shallots are completely done, and garlic softens. Add all spices and cook for 2 minutes and mix well.

2. Roughly chop tomatoes and add to the pan with 2 tablespoons water. Cook on low medium until sauce thickens. Add cooked chickpeas and mix well. Season.

3. Add the mixture on top of the toasted bread and add olives. Serve and enjoy.

BREAKFAST HASH

Cook Time: 1 hour

Servings: 6

Ingredients:

- 1 large sweet potato, peeled and diced
- 3 russet potatoes, peeled and diced
- 1 tablespoon garlic powder
- 1 tablespoon onion powder
- 1 teaspoon dried thyme
- 1/4 cup + 1 teaspoon olive oil
- 1 onion, diced
- 5 garlic cloves, minced
- Salt and pepper, to taste

Instructions:

1. Add potatoes, 1/4 cup olive oil, and spices to a bowl and mix well. Bake in a casserole dish at 450 F for 50 minutes. Stir every 20 minutes.
2. Add olive oil in a skillet and cook onion and garlic for 8 minutes — season to taste.
3. Add potatoes to the onion/garlic mixture and mix well to combine — Cook for 1-2 minutes.
4. Serve and enjoy.

SPINACH ARTICHOKE QUICHE

Cook Time: 1 hour

Servings: 4

Ingredients:

- 2 large tortillas
- 1 tablespoon coconut oil
- 2 garlic cloves, minced
- 1/2 onion, chopped
- 2 cups spinach
- 1/2 cup nutritional yeast
- 14 oz. soft tofu
- 14 oz. can artichokes, drained and chopped
- 1 teaspoon Dijon mustard
- 1 teaspoon dried basil
- 1 lemon juice
- 1/2 teaspoon turmeric
- 1/4 teaspoon pepper
- 1/4 teaspoon salt

Instructions:

1. Preheat the oven to 350 F and grease a pie dish with oil.

2. Cut tortillas in half and arrange on the pie dish — Bake for 15 minutes.

3. Heat oil in a pan. Add onion and cook for 5 minutes. Add garlic and cook for 2 minutes. Add spinach and cook until wilted. Remove.

4. Add spices, yeast, tofu, and lemon juice to a blender. Blend until smooth. Add onion mixture and artichokes to the blender and blend until mixed.

5. Transfer the mixture to the pie pan. Bake at 350F for 45 minutes. Serve and enjoy.

FRIED TOFU

Cook Time: 20 minutes

Servings: 4

Ingredients:

- 1 block firm tofu, drained
- 1 tablespoon vegan butter
- Salt and pepper, to taste

Instructions:

1. Cut tofu into 4 thick slices. Cut off the corners of tofu to make a circle.
2. Melt butter in a pan over medium heat. Add tofu slices in a single layer. Fry until light brown on one side, flip and fry on the other side.
3. Remove and place on plates. Garnish and serve.

BREAKFAST TURMERIC TOFU

Cook Time: 15 minutes

Servings: 8

Ingredients:

- 2 packs (16 oz. each) firm tofu, packed in water
- 2 1/2 tablespoon nutritional yeast
- 1 1/4 teaspoon granulated garlic
- 2 tablespoons vegan margarine
- 1 1/4 teaspoon granulated onion
- 1/8 teaspoon turmeric
- 3/4 teaspoon sea salt

- 1/2 teaspoon black pepper

Instructions:

1. Drain water from the tofu. Add margarine to a skillet and turn the heat to medium. Add tofu and mix well.

2. Add onion, garlic, turmeric, salt and pepper to the pan. Mix and cook for 5 minutes on medium heat. Add yeast. Continue to cook until done.

3. Serve and enjoy!

DELI-STYLE VEGAN CREAM CHEESE BOWLS

Cook Time: 10 minutes

Servings: 2 cups

Ingredients:

- 8 1/2 oz. firm silken tofu
- 1 tablespoon ume plum vinegar
- 1 tablespoon white wine vinegar
- 1/2 teaspoon garlic powder
- 2 tablespoons white onion, minced
- 2 tablespoons red bell pepper, seeded and minced
- 2 tablespoons carrot, minced
- 2 tablespoons cucumber, minced
- 1 teaspoon sea salt

Instructions:

1. Drain water from tofu. Mix vinegars, tofu, salt and garlic powder in a blender and blend until smooth.
2. Transfer to a bowl and add the veggies. Serve and enjoy.

CARDAMOM AND PEACH QUINOA PORRIDGE

Cook Time: 20 minutes

Servings: 2

Ingredients:

- 1/3 cup porridge oats
- 1/2 cup quinoa
- 4 cardamom pods
- 2 peaches, cut into slices
- 1 teaspoon maple syrup
- 8 1/2 oz. almond milk

Instructions:

1. Add cardamom, oats and quinoa to a pan with 9 oz. water and 3 1/2 oz. milk. Bring to a boil and cook for 15 minutes.
2. Add the remaining milk and cook for 5 minutes. Remove the cardamom pods, divide the mixture among bowls and add peaches and maple syrup. Serve and enjoy.

BANANA SMASH OATMEAL

Ingredients

- 1/4 cup antiquated oats
- 1/4 teaspoon cinnamon
- 1/2 cup in addition to 1 tablespoon almond milk, unsweetened
- 1 formula Roasted Banana Smash

Directions

1. Make the Roasted Banana Smash formula.
2. Meanwhile, add the initial 3 fixings to a pot and heat to the point of boiling.
3. Diminish heat to a low bubble and cook 5 minutes, or adhere to the directions on the oat's.
4. Expel from warmth and mix in the simmered banana crush, being certain to include all the sweet squeezes.

SIX PLANTS BASED OIL-FREE SALAD DRESSING

Ingredients

- Tamari Vinaigrette
- 1/4 cup tamari
- 1/4 cup balsamic or red wine vinegar
- 2 teaspoons Dijon mustard
- 1001 Islands
- 6 tablespoons luxurious tofu
- 3 tablespoons stone ground mustard
- 3 tablespoons ketchup
- 1 teaspoon crisply pressed lemon juice
- touch of salt
- touch of naturally ground pepper
- Agave Mustard
- 1/4 cup stone ground mustard
- 1/4 cup smooth tofu
- 3 tablespoons agave syrup
- touch of salt, or to taste
- touch of naturally ground dark pepper, or to taste
- Strawberry Vinaigrette
- 4 huge strawberries

- 1 tablespoon red wine vinegar
- 2 tablespoons agave syrup
- touch of naturally ground dark pepper
- Smooth Italian
- 6 tablespoons delicate, smooth tofu
- 4 tablespoons water
- 2 teaspoons new crushed lemon juice
- 1/2 teaspoons every garlic powder, onion powder, oregano chips, rosemary drops, basil pieces, and salt
- touch of newly ground dark pepper
- Sesame umami
- 1/4 cup tamari or soy sauce
- 2 tablespoons toasted sesame seeds
- 2 tablespoons rice vinegar
- 2 tablespoons water
- 1 huge clove finely squashed garlic

Directions

1. Tamari Vinaigrette: Whisk and blend in with a plate of mixed greens.
2. 1001 Islands: Puree utilizing submersion blender or whisk energetically until smooth.
3. Agave Mustard: Puree utilizing submersion blender or whisk energetically until smooth.

4. Strawberry Vinaigrette: Mix in nourishment processor or heartbeat in a rapid blender to hold surface whenever wanted.

5. Velvety Italian: Puree tofu and water utilizing a little nourishment processor or drenching blender at that point beat mix in different fixings to hold bits of shading from herb pieces.

6. Sesame umami: Toast sesame seeds in a skillet over medium-high warmth until they pop, at that point granulate seeds in flavor processor and whisk together with different fixings.

FUSION LUNCH BURRITOS

Ingredients

- 18 rice paper wrappers
- 8 ounces dark colored rice noodles, suggest Annie Chun's Maifun Brown Rice Noodles
- 5 ounces blended child greens, natural if conceivable
- 1 avocado
- 1 cucumber
- 2 chime peppers, your decision of shading
- 2 cups destroyed carrots
- 2 cups destroyed purple cabbage
- 1 (16 ounces) bundle firm or excessively firm square of tofu

- Veggie lover sans oil plate of mixed greens dressing – your decision

Directions

1. Prepare rice noodles as per bundle guidelines and afterward channel.
2. Peel and cut avocado, cucumber, and chime peppers into matchstick width strips.
3. Prepare tofu boards as portrayed in this formula, without the marinade, and afterward cut into matchstick width strips.
4. Add the vegetable fillings to an enormous bowl, at that point prepare and cover generously with the vegetarian sans oil serving of mixed greens dressing of your decision.
5. Prepare moves independently by submerging each sheet of rice wrapper in turn in a bowl of warm water for 10 seconds, at that point place on a cutting board or other clean level work surface.
6. Layer an even measure of plate of mixed greens filling crosswise over lower third of rice wrapper, leaving room on sides to fold edges for your burrito spring rolls.
7. Layer an even measure of tofu strips and rice noodles over plate of mixed greens filling, at that point overlay over edge folds and fold your burritos into completely encased cylinders.

8. The fixings recorded should make around 18 completed rolls. Spot completed moves on a serving plate, and be certain not to stack them, as they will stay together.

Eat, grin, and feel sound!

AVOCADO HUMMUS BOWL

Ingredients

- 1/2 ready avocado, stripped, pitted, and thickly cut
- 1/2 cup chickpeas (from a 15-ounce can), depleted and washed
- 1/2 medium estimated cucumber, meagerly cut
- 2/3 cup grape or cherry tomatoes
- 1 cup child carrots
- 10 spinach leaves, well-cleaned
- 1/3 cup clean eating hummus, any assortment, locally acquired or handcrafted
- 2 tablespoons pumpkin or shelled sunflower seeds, discretionary
- 1/4 teaspoon genuine or ocean salt
- 1/4 teaspoon dark pepper

Directions

1. Line a bowl with spinach leaves, layering if vital.
2. Add avocado cuts to one corner, chickpeas to another, grape tomatoes to another, and infant carrots to another.
3. Add hummus to the inside and top with sunflower or pumpkin seeds, if utilizing.
4. Sprinkle entire dish with salt and pepper and appreciate!

5. This is extraordinary for a to-go lunch when made in a compact holder with a top.

SLOW COOKER PUMPKIN CHILI

Ingredients

- 1 onion, diced
- 2 (14 ounces) jars squashed tomatoes
- 2 (14 ounces) jars dark beans, depleted
- 1 carrot, destroyed
- 1 chime pepper, diced
- 1 jalapeno, veins and seeds expelled and minced
- 2 cloves garlic, minced
- 1 1/2 cups pumpkin puree
- 1 cups low sodium vegetable soup
- 2 tablespoons stew powder
- 1 teaspoon pumpkin pie flavor
- 1 teaspoon Kosher salt
- 1/2 teaspoon dark pepper

Directions

1. Add everything to your moderate cooker and mix to consolidate.
2. Cook on low for 5 to 6 hours or high for 2 to 3 hours. Present with a bit of Greek yogurt or bested with avocado cuts.

BUTTERNUT SQUASH & AND CRANBERRY QUINOA SALAD

Ingredients

- 3 cups butternut squash, diced little
- 5 tablespoons extra-virgin olive oil
- 2 cups cooked quinoa
- 1/2 cup dried cranberries
- 1/3 cup pecans pieces
- 1 tablespoon newly slashed basil
- 1/4 teaspoon legitimate or ocean salt
- 1/4 teaspoon dark pepper

Directions

1. Pour 3 tablespoons of extra-virgin olive oil into a medium pot. Sauté the squash over medium-low warmth until cooked through and delicate.
2. In an enormous bowl, blend the cooked squash, quinoa, cranberries, pecans, basil, salt, pepper, and the staying 2 tablespoons of additional virgin olive oil.

HERBED WILD RICE STUFFED POTATOES

Ingredients

- 4 enormous chestnut potatoes
- 2 tablespoons olive oil, partitioned
- 1/2 teaspoon coarse ocean salt, partitioned
- 1 shallot, minced
- 1 clove garlic, minced
- 4 cups infant spinach
- 1 cup wild rice or wild rice mix, cooked by bundle headings
- 2 tablespoons crisp slashed parsley
- 2 tablespoons crisp slashed basil

- 1 teaspoon minced chives
- 1 tablespoon crisp lemon juice
- 1/4 teaspoon new ground dark pepper

Directions

1. Preheat stove to 350 degrees F. Coat the potatoes in 1/2 tablespoon of the oil and rub with a large portion of the salt. Lay on a preparing sheet and heat for 1/2 hour. Expel from the stove and prick with a fork, and set back in the broiler. Keep heating until potatoes are delicate, around 45 minutes more.

2. While the potatoes are preparing, make the filling.

3. Heat the rest of the oil in a skillet over medium warmth. Include the shallots and garlic and cook until delicate. Include the spinach and cook until simply withered. Mix in the cooked rice and mood killer the warmth. Mix in the herbs, lemon juice, staying salt and pepper.

4. When the potatoes are done, they divided each into equal parts. Stuff each with about a half cup of the rice blend and serve.

SPICY KALE SALAD WITH CHICKPEAS AND MAPLE DIJON DRESSING

Ingredients

For the Salad:

- 1 (15 ounces) can chickpeas, depleted and flushed
- 1/2 teaspoon cayenne pepper
- 1/4 teaspoon red pepper pieces
- 3 cups kale, generally cleaved
- 1/2 cup carrot, destroyed
- 1/2 cup red onion, cut into slight strips
- 1 jalapeno pepper, cut into small strips (for additional zest, utilize a habanero pepper!)

For the Dressing:

- 1/4 cup apple juice vinegar
- 2 tablespoons unadulterated maple syrup
- 1 tablespoon dijon mustard
- 1 teaspoon orange get-up-and-go

Guidelines

For the Salad:

1. In a medium bowl, join the chickpeas, cayenne pepper, and red pepper pieces. Hurl well to cover the chickpeas in the flavors.

2. 2In an enormous bowl, consolidate the chickpeas and the rest of the plate of mixed greens fixings. Prepare well to join and place the blended plate of mixed greens into serving bowls. Sprinkle with around 3 teaspoons of dressing and serve.

For the Dressing:

1. Combine all fixings and whisk well. Let sit for 5 minutes. Give the dressing a brisk mix before sprinkling over the serving of mixed greens.

GLUTEN-FREE MANGO AND BLACK BEAN TACOS

Ingredients

- 2 Roma tomatoes, diced little
- 2 tablespoons red onion diced little
- 1/4 cup orange ringer pepper, diced little
- 1 tablespoon lime juice
- 2 tablespoons new cilantro, hacked
- 1/2 teaspoon Kosher salt
- 1 (15 ounces) can dark beans, depleted and washed
- 1/4 cup vegetable soup
- 6 gluten-free corn tortillas
- 1 ready mango, cut into strips
- 1 avocado, pit and strip expelled, cut into little pieces

Directions

2. In a blending bowl, consolidate the tomatoes, onion, chime pepper, lime juice, cilantro, and salt. Blend to consolidate. Spread and put aside to rest.

3. Meanwhile, in a little bot, heat the dark beans and vegetable juices, bring to a stew and cook for around 5 minutes. Expel from warm and delicately squash, making a

point to leave a few beans entire and the blend exceptionally stout.

4. Heat a large skillet on high warmth, an iron fry dish works extraordinarily! At the point when the skillet is hot, include one corn tortilla. Cook for around 30 seconds, or until caramelized and go over to cook the second side for around 30 seconds. Spot the seared tortilla on a warm plate. Rehash with outstanding tortillas.

5. Place the tortiallas on a level surface and spread with the dark beans. Top the beans with mango and avocado. Spoon the tomato blend on top. Serve and appreciate!

SPICY KALE SALAD WITH CHICKPEAS AND MAPLE DIJON DRESSING

Ingredients

For the Salad:

- 1 (15 ounce) can chickpeas, depleted and washed
- 1/2 teaspoon cayenne pepper
- 1/4 teaspoon red pepper pieces
- 3 cups kale, generally cleaved
- 1/2 cup carrot, destroyed
- 1/2 cup red onion, cut into slender strips
- 1 jalapeno pepper, cut into slender strips (for additional zest, utilize a habanero pepper!)

For the Dressing:

- 1/4 cup apple juice vinegar
- 2 tablespoons unadulterated maple syrup
- 1 tablespoon dijon mustard
- 1 teaspoon orange get-up-and-go

Directions For the Salad:

1. In a medium bowl, consolidate the chickpeas, cayenne pepper, and red pepper drops. Hurl well to cover the chickpeas in the flavors.

2. In a huge bowl, join the chickpeas and the rest of the plate of mixed greens fixings. Prepare well to consolidate and put the blended plate of mixed greens into serving bowls. Sprinkle with around 3 teaspoons of dressing and serve.

For the Dressing:

1. Combine all fixings and whisk well. Let sit for 5 minutes. Give the dressing a snappy mix before sprinkling over the plate of mixed greens.

OLD-FASHIONED POTATO SALAD

Ingredients

- 2 pounds red potatoes, with skins

- 1 tablespoon fit or ocean salt

- 1/2 cup diced celery

- 1/2 cup diced red onion

- 1/2 paprika (for decorate), discretionary

- Plant-Based Mayonnaise

- 1 cup crue cashews + 2 cups water for drenching

- 3/4 cup water

- 2 tablespoons newly crushed lemon juice

- 2 tablespoons white wine vinegar
- 1 teaspoon garlic powder
- 1/2 teaspoon onion powder
- 1 teaspoon ocean salt
- 1/2 teaspoon dark pepper
- 2 tablespoons Dijon mustard
- 2 tablespoons entire grain mustard
- 1/3 cup hacked dill weed

Directions

2. Wash and clean potatoes, cut into 3D shapes, around 1-1/2 inches. Include potatoes and 1 tablespoon salt to an enormous pot, totally spread potatoes with water and heat to the point of boiling. Lessen warmth to a low-bubble. Cook until potatoes are delicate when penetrated with a fork, 15-20 minutes. Channel potatoes, spread and put in a safe spot.

3. While potatoes are cooking, add cashews to a huge bowl, spread with 2 cups water and permit to set 15 minutes. Channel and flush cashews.

4. Include flushed cashews and 3/4 cup water to a blender, beat until a smooth consistency. Empty blend into a blending bowl.

5. Include remaining fixings, aside from red onions and celery, to the cashew/water blend. Rush until all around

consolidated. Note: mayo will thicken up following a few hours, and is best when made the prior night.

6. Add onions and celery to potatoes, hurl to join.

7. Pour around 1 cup mayo over the potatoes, hurl to join. Include extra mayo for a definitive smooth potato serving of mixed greens. Include extra salt whenever wanted. Softly sprinkle the top with paprika.

8. Cover and refrigerate 2-3 hours before serving.

THREE BEAN SALAD

This dish is unquestionable requirements have at any braai however can likewise be presented with flame-broiled chicken bosoms as a light summer supper alternative!

Recipe serves6 - 8

Preparation time20 minutes

Ingredients

- 1 red onion, finely cut
- 1 tin chickpeas, depleted and flushed
- 1 tin kidney beans, drained and washed
- 250 g cherry tomatoes, divided
- 150 g green beans, toped and followed
- 30 g rocket, washed
- 30 ml KNORR Light Greek Salad Dressing

Dircctions

1. Place every one of the fixings together in a bowl and blend well to join.
2. Serve right away.

GREEK CHICKEN, TOMATO & FETA BAKE

This simple-to-make heated chicken and feta dish will dazzle family, companions and fans the same.

Recipe serves4-6

Preparation time15 minutes

Cooking time45 minutes

Ingredients

- 500 g Baby potatoes, divided
- 6 Small chicken thighs on the bone, skin on
- 1 KNORR Brown Onion Gravy
- 1 tsp Robertsons Paprika
- 2 Red onions, cut into eighths
- 1 Red pepper, cut into strips
- 1 Yellow pepper, cut into strips
- 3 Garlic cloves, squashed
- 2 tbsp Olive oil
- 1 tsp Robertsons Origanum
- Robertsons Salt and Pepper
- 200 g Tin diced tomatoes
- 12 Black olives

- Chopped level leaf parsley
- 250 ml Feta cheddar, disintegrated

Directions

1. Preheat broiler to 200°C.
2. In an enormous container of bubbling water cook potatoes for 10 minutes.
3. Drain and put aside to cool.
4. Place chicken in an enormous preparing dish.
5. Sprinkle with KNORR Brown Onion Gravy and paprika.
6. Add onions, peppers, garlic and potatoes.
7. Drizzle with oil, sprinkle with origanum and season well. Bake for 30 minutes. Add tomatoes and olives, seasoning chicken with the juices.
8. Cook for 15 additional minutes.
9. Serve sprinkled with parsley and feta cheddar.

BUTTERNUT & LEEK SOUP

Customary butternut soup plans are an absolute necessity have on your winter feast organizer, so here's a delectable one made with leek and green apple.

Recipe serves4-6

Preparation time10 minutes

Cooking time40 minutes

Ingredients

- 15-milliliter oil
- 3 Leeks, cut
- ½ Onion slashed
- 1 kilogram Butternut, cubed
- 1 Green Apple, cored and slashed
- ½ teaspoon Black pepper
- 1 KNORR Vegetable Stock Pot
- 300 millimeter Milk
- 200 millimeter Water
- 1 A swirl of Cream to serve

•

Directions

1. Heat oil in an enormous pot; include leeks and onion and sauté until they mellow.
2. Add butternut, apple and dark pepper.
3. Add KNORR Vegetable Stock Pot, milk and water, and add to the soup blend.
4. Simmer for 25-30 min until the butternut is delicate.
5. Once cooked, place in a liquidizer and puree until smooth.
6. Serve with a whirl of cream and topping gently with dark pepper.

CHICKEN VINAIGRETTE

Yield: 4 servings

TIME Prep: 30 min. Cook: 30 min.

Ingredients

- 1 oven/fryer chicken (3 pounds), cut up and skin expelled
- 1 teaspoon vegetable oil
- Salt and pepper to taste
- 1 huge onion, hacked

- 1 garlic clove, minced
- 4 medium carrots, cut
- 4 medium red potatoes, split
- 1/2 cup water
- 1 tablespoon minced new parsley
- 1 teaspoon dried basil
- 1/2 teaspoon chicken bouillon granules
- Pinch dried thyme
- 1/2 cup each cleaved sweet red and yellow pepper (1-inch pieces)
- 2 green onions cut

    1/4 cup juice or red wine vinegar

Direction

1. In a nonstick skillet, dark-colored chicken in oil. Sprinkle with salt and pepper. Expel and keep warm. In the drippings, saute onion and garlic until delicate.

2. Mix in the carrots, potatoes, water, and seasonings; top with chicken.

3. Reduce heat; spread and stew for 25 minutes, mixing every so often. Mix in extra water if necessary. Include peppers and green onions.

4. Spread and cook until chicken juices run clear and vegetables are delicate around 5 minutes. Mix in vinegar; heat through.

HEARTY BEEF STEW WITH MUSHROOMS AND MASH

Use red wine, button mushrooms, and cubed beef to make this tasty stew ideal for a hearty family feast.

- Recipe serves4
- Preparation time10 minutes
- Cooking time35 minutes

Ingredients

- 150 g Pickling onions, peeled
- 15 ml oil
- 3 ml crushed garlic
- 500 g Cubed lean beef
- 100 ml Red wine (optional)
- 1 Red pepper, cut into strips
- 150 g Button mushrooms, whole
- 1 KNORR Hearty Beef Stew with Rosemary Dry Cook-in-Sauce
- 400 ml of cold water
- 45 ml Chopped fresh Italian flat-leaf parsley
- 350 g potatoes, cubed and boiled
- 50 ml Milk
- 20 g Stork Margarine

Method

1. In a large pot, brown onions in oil and add garlic and beef cubes.

2. Fry until the meat is browned, then add the wine, red pepper and mushrooms and fry for 2 min.

3. Add 400 ml cold water to the pot and stir in the contents of the KNORR Hearty Beef Stew sachet.

4. Bring to the boil while stirring.

5. Simmer uncovered for 20 min, stirring occasionally and add parsley.

6. Prepare mashed potatoes by mixing potato, milk and Stork margarine.

7. Serve stew with potato as a side dish.

EASY SEAFOOD BREYANI WITH PRAWNS, HAKE AND CALAMARI

Use prawns, hake, and calamari to make this unusual seafood breyani dish.

Recipe serves4

Preparation time10 minutes

Cooking time20 minutes

Ingredients

- 2 tomatoes, cubed
- 30 ml Fresh coriander, chopped
- 300 g Hake fillet, cubed
- 200 g Prawns, deveined and shelled
- 800 ml Water
- 1 box KNORR Rice Mate Mild Breyani
- 15 ml of oil
- 200 g Calamari rings

Method

1. In a large saucepan, fry the hake and calamari in oil for 3 min.

2. Add the sachet of seasoning mix, 800 ml hot water, and the uncooked rice and bring to the boil.

3. Reduce the heat and simmer for 15 min, stirring occasionally.

4. Stir in the prawns and tomato, and simmer for a further 5 min.

5. Top with chopped coriander.

PORTUGUESE-STYLE CHICKEN

A nice and spicy chicken dish with the flavors of Portugal all cooked together in one bag!

Recipe serves4-6

Preparation time15 minutes

Cooking time45 minutes

Ingredients

- 1 KNORR Cook-in-Bag Spicy Roast Chicken

- 10 skinless chicken thighs

- 1 red pepper, sliced

- 1 punnet mange tout

- 700g sweet potatoes, cubed with skin intact

- 15 ml of lemon juice

- 1 clove roughly chopped garlic

- 5 ml Robertsons Portuguese Chicken Spice

Method

1. Preheat oven to 180°C.

2. Place chicken thighs, red pepper, mange tout, sweet potatoes, lemon juice, garlic and Portuguese Chicken Spice into the cooking bag.

3. Sprinkle the seasoning mix inside the bag, hold the bag closed and roll gently to coat the ingredients evenly.

4. Place the cooking bag onto a baking tray.

5. Knot the bag loosely to seal and pierce the top of the bag 3 times with a knife for the steam to escape.

6. Place the baking tray in the center of the oven and bake for 40-45 minutes. Ensure that the grill is off at all times.

7. Cut the bag open and transfer to a serving dish with any sauce that is in the bag.

CHEF WENDY

Cooking With Lentils

Dried lentils are a fantastic ingredient when it comes to 'stretching' family meals - they're inexpensive, packed with fiber, and so versatile because they have a mild, neutral taste that can be combined with many interesting flavors to create memorable and comforting dishes! They're lovely in stews, curries, soups and bakes, and you can also use them to make excellent warm winter salads.

BUYING LENTILS

- Ordinary brown lentils cost very little and can be found in all supermarkets, in the aisle where the dried beans and pulses are.

- You can also use whole green lentils, or split red or yellow lentils.

- If you're in a hurry, you can use tinned, drained lentils in any of the recipes below (these are already cooked).

HOW TO COOK LENTILS

- Lentils do not need to be soaked before they are cooked, although by soaking them ahead you can reduce the cooking time by about half.

- First, rinse the lentils very well in a sieve to remove any little stones or shriveled lentils.

- Put 1.5 liters cold water into a pot and add 2 cups of dried lentils.

- Bring the pot quickly to the boil, and then turn down the heat and cook, uncovered, over medium-low heat, until the lentils are soft.

- How long they will take to cook depends on the type of lentil. Split red lentils take about 20 minutes, and form a creamy purée, making them ideal for thickening soups and curries. Brown lentils take about 30 minutes, and green lentils a little longer.

- Keep checking the lentils to see whether they are done to your liking. They should be tender you're eating them in a salad or a side dish, and a little softer if they're going into a soup, stew or curry.

- Don't let the lentils get mushy (except if you're cooking split red lentils), and watch the pot closely, so it doesn't dry out.

- Immediately tip the contents of the pot into a large sieve or colander set over the sink, and allow draining for 3-4 minutes. Now add some fabulous flavors…

- You can add some flavoring agents to the boiling water if you like – for example, a slice of onion, a few bay leaves, a cinnamon stick, curry leaves or similar whole spices. Discard these when you drain the lentils.

- Don't add acidic ingredients such as lemon, tomatoes or vinegar to the pot, as these may slow down the cooking process.

HOW TO FLAVOUR LENTILS

- Tip your drained, hot lentils back into the pot in which they boiled and add a Knorr Vegetable or Chicken Stock Pot. Stir until the contents of the stockpot have dissolved. This will add a lovely depth of flavor to the lentils, and will also help season them.

- You can now go ahead and creatively use the cooked lentils as a basic ingredient in a variety of dishes (see our great easy recipes below).

- Or you can create a warm or cold dish to serve on its own as a main course or a side dish.

Here are some other ingredients that go beautifully with a warm or cold lentil salad:

- Cooked beetroot, roasted peppers, roasted butternut

- Chopped fresh herbs such as parsley, chives, mint, basil, spring onions & coriander

- Salad leaves such as wild rocket and watercress

- Feta cheese, Halloumi cheese, goat's cheese and ricotta

- Raw or oven-roasted cherry tomatoes

- Finely chopped cucumber, carrots, peppers and baby marrows

- Garlic, lemon, lemon zest, white-wine vinegar, mustard, olive oil

- Crispy bacon bits

- Toasted sunflower or pumpkin seeds

- Knorr salad dressings of your choice

To make a hot lentil dish, add all or any of the following ingredients:

- A few pinches, to taste, of curry powder, cumin, powdered coriander, cinnamon, chilli powder, turmeric and similar warming spices

- Chopped tomatoes, tinned or fresh

- Fresh chillies, ginger and garlic

- Fried onions and green peppers

- Cooked potato cubes

- Tinned chickpeas or beans

- Cooked vegetables such as cauliflower, baby marrow, butternut, spinach and brinjal

BAKE DINNER

Total Time: 1 hr 25 min Prep: 10 min Cook: 1 hr 15 min

Ingredients

- 1 whole chicken, 4 lbs, washed and patted dry
- 2 cloves garlic
- Salt
- Pepper
- Fresh herbs: tarragon, rosemary or thyme
- 6 tablespoons butter
- 1 onion, peeled and halved
- 3 parsnips, peeled and chopped into 3 inch pieces
- 3 carrots, peeled and chopped into 3 inch pieces
- 3 potatoes, quartered
- 2 tablespoons olive oil
- Gravy:
- Splash white wine
- 1 cup chicken stock
- Chopped fresh herbs
- Salt
- Pepper

Directions

1. Preheat oven to 425 degrees. Remove giblet bag from chicken's cavity, season cavity well with salt and pepper.

2. Chop up garlic with salt and herbs. Mash garlic mixture with butter. Slide butter mixture under the breast skin of the chicken and next to legs, stuff cavity with onion and whole herbs.

3. Place chicken into roasting pan. Roast for 30 minutes at 425 and then reduce heat to 375. In a large bowl, toss vegetables with olive oil and add to roasting pan. Roast chicken for another 40 minutes. Occasionally baste the chicken with pan juices.

4. To check the chicken for doneness, prick leg with knife and press to see juices. If the juices run clear, then the chicken is done. Remove from the oven and let sit for 15 minutes.

5. Remove roasted vegetables to a side dish and keep warm in the oven. Place roasting pan on a stove burner over medium heat. Add wine and chicken stock. Stir and rub the bottom of the pan to scrape up brown bits, bring to a simmer and season with salt and pepper. Serve hot

VEGETABLE FRIED RICE RECIPES

This is a basic recipe for fried rice that you can add to as desired. If adding other ingredients, increase the number of eggs to 3. Need a bit of help? Here are step by step photo instructions showing how to make basic fried rice.

Prep Time: 5 minutes **Cook Time**: 10 minutes **Total Time**: 15 minutes **Yield**: Serves 4 to 6

Ingredients

- 1 - 2 green onions, as desired

- 2 large eggs

- 1 teaspoon salt

- Pepper to taste

- 4 tablespoons oil for stir-frying, or as needed

- 4 cups cold cooked rice

- 1 - 2 tablespoons light soy sauce or oyster sauce, as desired

Directions:

1. Wash and finely chop the green onion. Lightly beat the eggs with the salt and pepper. Heat a wok or frying pan and add 2 tablespoons oil.

2. When the oil is hot, add the eggs, cook, stirring, until they are lightly scrambled but not too dry. Remove the eggs and clean out the pan.

3. Add 2 tablespoons oil. Add the rice. Stir-fry for a few minutes, using chopsticks or a wooden spoon to break it apart. Stir in the soy sauce or oyster sauce as desired.

4. When the rice is heated through, add the scrambled egg back into the pan. Mix thoroughly. Stir in the green onion. Serve hot.

MEXICAN HEALTHY DINNERS

Minutes to Prepare: 10 Minutes To Cook: 5 Number Of Servings: 8

Ingredients

- 2 c. fat free chicken broth
- 1 - 15 oz can white beans OR fat free refried beans (drained)
- 1 - 15 oz can S&W black beans (drained)
- 1 - 15 oz can S&W Stewed Mexican Recipe Tomatoes (barely drained)
- 1 - 15 oz can medium pitted olives (drained)
- 1.5 cups golden hominy
- 1 - 7 oz can diced green chilies
- 1 garlic clove, minced
- 2 tbsp chili powder

Directions

1. Open all the cans. Drain the beans and olives, and drain a small amount of liquid off the tomatoes. Pour all the ingredients into a large saucepan. Mince the garlic and add the pot. Season to taste
2. Makes 8 - 1 cup servings of about 153 calories each!

3. Lots of good, healthy nutrients but it is pretty high in sodium.

4. Goes particularly well with a bit of shredded cheddar cheese or a few avocado slices if you have a few more calories to spare for your meal

Number of Servings: 8

FAIRHAVEN FISH CHOWDER

Ingredients

- 3 lbs. (cod, haddock, hake, halibut)
- 1 quart diced potatoes
- 1/4 teaspoon ground cloves (optional)
- 1 tablespoon thyme
- 1 tablespoon marjoram
- 1 bay leaf
- 2 cloves garlic (optional)
- 1 or 2 onions, chopped (optional)
- 1/2 lb lean salt pork, diced
- 1 1/2 cups canned diced tomatoes
- 1 tablespoon sage
- 5 soda crackers (Pilot or Milk Lunch type)
- salt and pepper, to taste

Directions:

1. Whether prepared in a Crock-Pot or on the stovetop for a winter evening's meal, or over the gas grill's side burner in the dog days of summer, this Fish Chowder is always good.

2. It can be made ahead, and is even better the next day! Unlike the traditional New England clam chowder, this version more resembles what has come to be known as Manhattan Style Clam Chowder.

3. This recipe is a famous Rhode Island recipe circa the early 1800s, which Mrs. Elizabeth Bumpus shared with friends while living in Fairhaven, Massachusetts in 1930.

PASTA SALAD

This pasta salad is a winner on all kinds of levels: quick to prep, delicious to eat and a Healthy Living recipe to boot.

Prep Time: 20min. Total Time 3hr. 20min. Servings 4 servings

Ingredients

- 16 ounces spiral-shaped pasta
- 1 cup cubed cooked chicken
- 1 cup Hellmann's mayonnaise
- 1 cup milk
- 1 cup frozen peas
- 1 cup finely diced celery
- 1 (1 ounce) package ranch dressing mix
- $\frac{1}{4}$ cup finely chopped onion
- 1 tablespoon dill weed
- $\frac{1}{2}$ cup sour cream

Directions

1. Cook pasta; drain.

2. Mix with the rest of the ingredients.

3. Chill overnight.

BUFFALO CHICKEN WINGS

Ingredients

- 10-12 chicken wings (2 1/2 lbs.)
- 1/4 to 3/4 cup hot pepper sauce
- 1/4 cup butter
- Vegetable or peanut oil (for frying)
- 4 cloves garlic, minced
- 1 shallot, minced (optional)
- 1 onion, finely minced (optional)
- pinch of sea salt

Directions

1. Fill a heavy-bottomed, deep-sided frying pan with at least 1 inch of oil and heat until temperature reaches 400°F.

2. Split the wings at each joint and discard tips. Rinse and pat dry with paper towels.

3. Meanwhile, in a small saucepan, melt butter over low heat with minced garlic. (Finely minced shallots or onions may optionally be added at the same time as the garlic.) If you prefer a smoother sauce, a stick blender may be used to smooth it out and blend in the flavors of the garlic, etc. When the garlic is a golden color, stir in the hot sauce. Add a pinch of salt.

4. When the oil is the correct temperature, carefully lower the wings into the hot oil using a slotted spoon or wire basket, and deep fry for about 12 minutes, or until wings are cooked and crispy.

5. Drain on paper towels. Toss with the hot sauce, coating several times to cover well.

6. Serving Suggestion: Serve with a side of extra hot sauce for dipping, and a bowl of Blue Cheese Dressing or Ranch dip and celery sticks.